PENDULUMS

FOR GUIDANCE & HEALING

Publisher & Creative Director: Nick Wells
Commissioning Editor: Polly Prior
Editorial Director: Catherine Taylor
Art Director: Mike Spender
Digital Design & Production: Chris Herbert

Special thanks to: Anna Groves, Dawn Laker, Frances Bodiam
and the artists who allowed us to reproduce their work.

FLAME TREE PUBLISHING
6 Melbray Mews, Fulham,
London SW6 3NS, United Kingdom
www.flametreepublishing.com

First published 2021

21 23 25 24 22
1 3 5 7 9 10 8 6 4 2

ISBN: 978-1-83964-201-2

A copy of the CIP data for this book is available from the British Library.

Printed in China | Created, Developed & Produced in the United Kingdom

PENDULUMS
FOR GUIDANCE & HEALING

Maggie & Nigel Percy

Foreword by Dr Patrick MacManaway

FLAME TREE
PUBLISHING

CONTENTS

FOREWORD

Dowsing is an ancient and perhaps universal art and skill, focusing our awareness and natural intuitive abilities to inform, help and guide us in every part of our life.

A very simple process, dowsing is easily learned and then patiently practised and refined as we become increasingly familiar, confident and adept with integrating it into daily usefulness.

Growing up in a family of dowsers, pendulums were scattered through the house like pens and pencils, and were regularly in use for guidance on issues big and small, from selecting cooking and baking ingredients and timings, to gardening matters of planting, soil enhancement and growing conditions. It was used for healthcare decisions, financial decisions, travel plans … an endless and constant help in navigating daily life in the most practical of ways.

Passing on the tradition in my own turn to my daughter, I found her from the outset demonstrating her ability and competence. When she was just six, she won a game of Trivial Pursuit against all assembled adults by dowsing the answers to the multiple-choice questions.

Through membership and service to the British Society of Dowsers and travels to visit dowsers around the world, I have met and been exposed to a huge range of dowsing applications, from mineral

and water exploration to civil, military and aviation engineering, as well as agricultural uses in the care of soils, plants and livestock. Because dowsing is a process guided by our mind, the uses and applications are limited only by our imagination.

Dowsers historically and culturally have used a variety of tools and methods and, as it is a natural process, sometimes no tools at all.

Often the choice of dowsing tool is dictated by the job or traditional practices in one or another area of dowsing interest, otherwise by the dowser's own personal preference.

The pendulum is perhaps the most convenient and versatile of dowsing tools, and can be simple to make with ordinary everyday materials, or finely crafted and exquisite. Any pendulum will do and we gravitate towards personal preference of weight, cord length, material and aesthetic. Ultimately, the best pendulum is the one in your hand.

Maggie and Nigel are long-serving and well-respected members of the dowsing community, and we are delighted and grateful to them for having assembled this comprehensive work on dowsing and pendulums.

Dr Patrick MacManaway
Past President, British Society of Dowsers

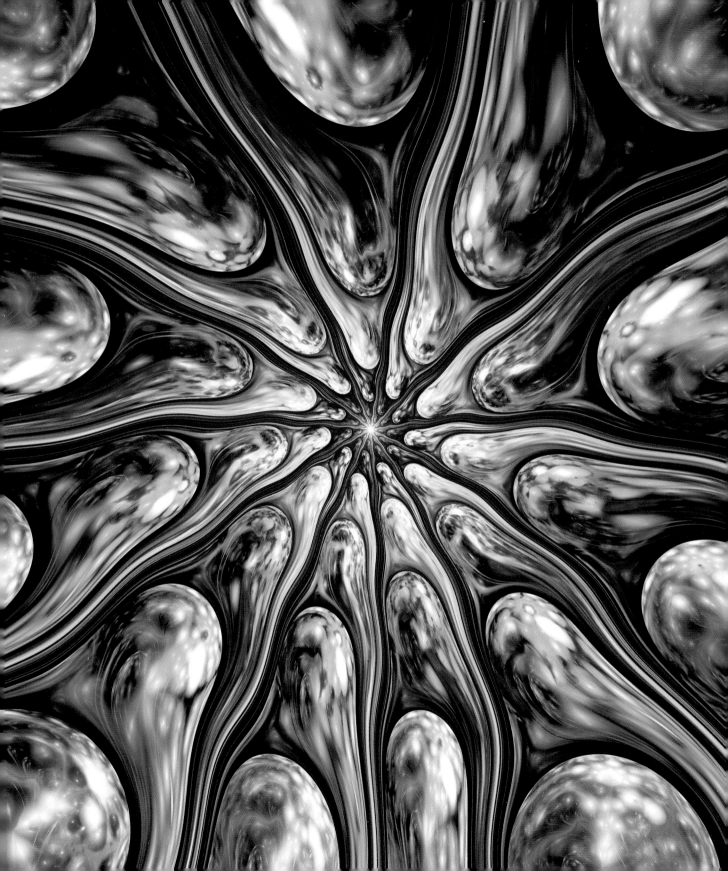

HARNESSING THE POWER WITHIN

We discovered the power of the pendulum in the 1990s. For us, the use of the pendulum became the gateway to exploring our intuition and natural healing abilities. It was fun and it challenged us to think in new ways. While we were applying ourselves to mastering its use, the pendulum led us to a more fulfilling way of life than we ever imagined.

Wow! You Can Do What?

Amazement is the natural reaction the first time anyone sees a pendulum in use. It seems simply magical to be able to find a lost object, make a major life choice or even heal an ailment using a weighted object suspended from a chain or string.

'There is more wisdom in your body than in your deepest philosophies.'

FRIEDRICH NIETZSCHE

As it turns out, a pendulum is *not* a magic wand, but the power it harnesses is nothing short of miraculous.

The pendulum taps into natural human abilities that lie dormant in all of us. Anyone can learn to use a pendulum for guidance or healing. The power within is waiting to be unleashed.

You Do not Need to Be Psychic

A few simple steps and you are on your way to getting answers to questions your brain cannot answer or to resolving the cause of a symptom. In this book, we give you the basics so you can get started right away using your pendulum. We also explore some of the many applications available to you once you begin to harness this innate power.

BEFORE YOU START

Before you pick up a pendulum, know this: using a pendulum is not a game. You are embarking on an empowering journey of self-discovery, and we urge you to act responsibly.

The Peter Parker Principle

'With great power comes great responsibility.' Uncle Ben's statement to Peter Parker in *Spider-Man* has become a proverb for guiding people in the appropriate use of power. It applies when you pick up a pendulum.

A pendulum is a tool of great power. Any power can be used for good or evil. Sometimes, evil can result from good intentions. So it is important to develop a sense of ethics to guide you when you take up the power of the pendulum. Even if you are simply having fun, be aware of the power you hold in your hand.

Use Your Power Wisely

The simplest way to know whether you are using your pendulum ethically is to use it for your own personal guidance and healing. If you want to use the pendulum to gather information about anyone else or to heal anyone else, you must get their permission first.

Dowsing is a simple and natural process, and is a universal human ability.

DR PATRICK MACMANAWAY

THE POWER OF PENDULUMS

Humans have always used the power of tools to make jobs easier. Power is usually seen as either natural or supernatural (magical). A lever used to move a heavy object is clearly a natural tool. A spell in the hands of a witch is considered magical, because it seems to have unexplainable power over natural processes. Is the power of the pendulum magical or natural?

Magical vs Natural Power

Whether you are using a pendulum for dowsing or healing, you are simply accessing natural human abilities. All humans have intuition. All humans have the ability to channel healing energy. A pendulum is not a magic wand. It is a simple, natural tool anyone can learn to use effectively.

On its own the pendulum 'knows nothing'. It may, however, present what you 'know' in an accessible form.

NAOMI OZANIEC

A Tool with Many Uses

A pendulum is defined as a weight suspended from a fixed point so that it can swing freely. Pendulums can be used in many different ways and have a variety of designs based on their purpose.

You have probably seen a pendulum swinging back and forth in an old grandfather clock. A hypnotist might use a shiny object as a pendulum while putting a subject into a trance state. In this book, we will

be talking about two other uses of pendulums: for guidance and healing. In both cases, the pendulum is a powerful tool for accomplishing your goals.

Dowsing: Getting Answers

When you use a pendulum for guidance, you are employing a technique called dowsing. Dowsing is a way of getting answers to questions that your rational mind cannot answer. Although sometimes said to be a psychic ability, dowsing is a natural skill that anyone can learn.

> For many years now, the pendulum has been a good friend and helper to me on my journeys of discovery into the spiritual world with its many different types of energy.
>
> WALTER LÜBECK

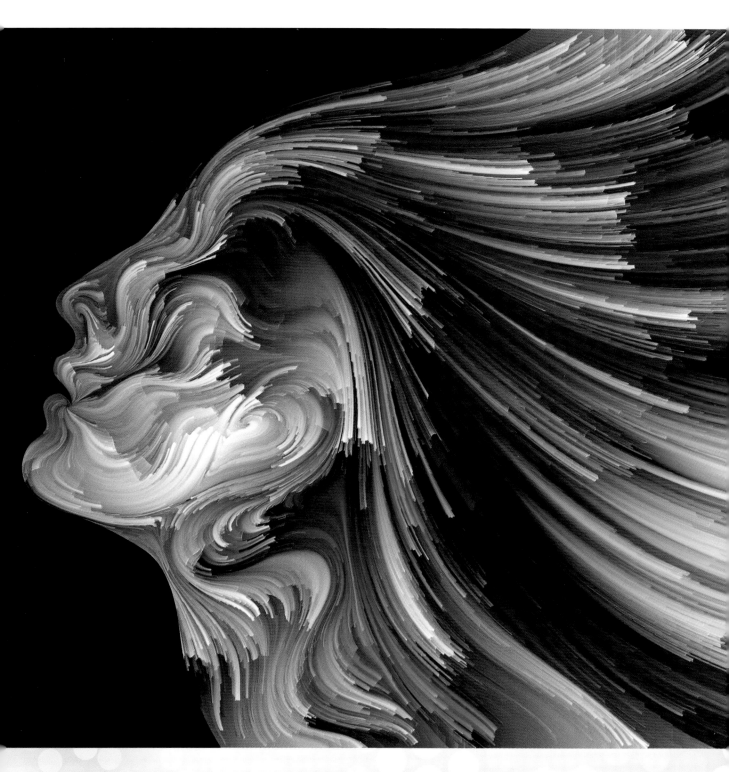

There are many times in life that you want or need to know what you should do. Your brain is very powerful for that purpose, but it functions best in rational, linear situations. What can you do if you need to 'know' an answer for which there are no rational or analytical steps? That is when you pick up your pendulum and dowse.

Pendulum Healing

Natural healing methods that do not have unpleasant or dangerous side effects have always been in great demand. There are many wonderful energy healing methods. Some have been used for centuries, like chi gong. Others, like reiki, are more recent. They all have the benefit of being safe and effective.

Pendulum healing is a modern energy healing method that uses the vibrational frequency of a pendulum to focus and channel the healing energy of the practitioner.

The Power Is in You!

Whether you are using a pendulum for guidance or healing, it is important to remember the power is not in the tool. It is in *you.*

When you take charge of your life, you become the pilot instead of the passenger. It is so empowering to expand your intelligence by accessing your intuition

> # The great mistake people will make when studying dowsing is to learn about it instead of learning it.
>
> TOM GRAVES

through dowsing. And when you commit to healing yourself or others with pendulum healing, you are claiming the ability to channel the life force, a power that is used in all natural healing methods.

A pendulum is a tool of empowerment. You step into your power when you choose to use it.

A HISTORY OF DOWSING & PENDULUMS

Dowsing has been used in various forms and for various tasks throughout history. It is something which anyone can do and was first written about some 400 years ago. Since then, dowsing has developed in many different ways and has been the subject of much speculation and experimentation.

Dowsing: A Natural Skill

Because dowsing is a simple, natural skill available to anyone, it was probably used for a considerable period of time before it was first written about. The first references to it occur in the sixteenth century. In 1556, a book on mining and smelting of ore, *De Re Metallica*, included a description of dowsing, as well as woodcuts showing dowsers at work identifying ore locations.

For a long time, dowsing was closely associated with mining. Although water dowsing slowly grew in prominence in the literature, such a useful skill had probably been familiar to many farmers for much longer than it has been written about. In 1897, Professor William Barrett published the results of an extensive scientific study that proved that water dowsing works.

Famous Pendulum Dowsers

Pendulum dowsing was popularized principally by French dowsers at the end of the nineteenth century.

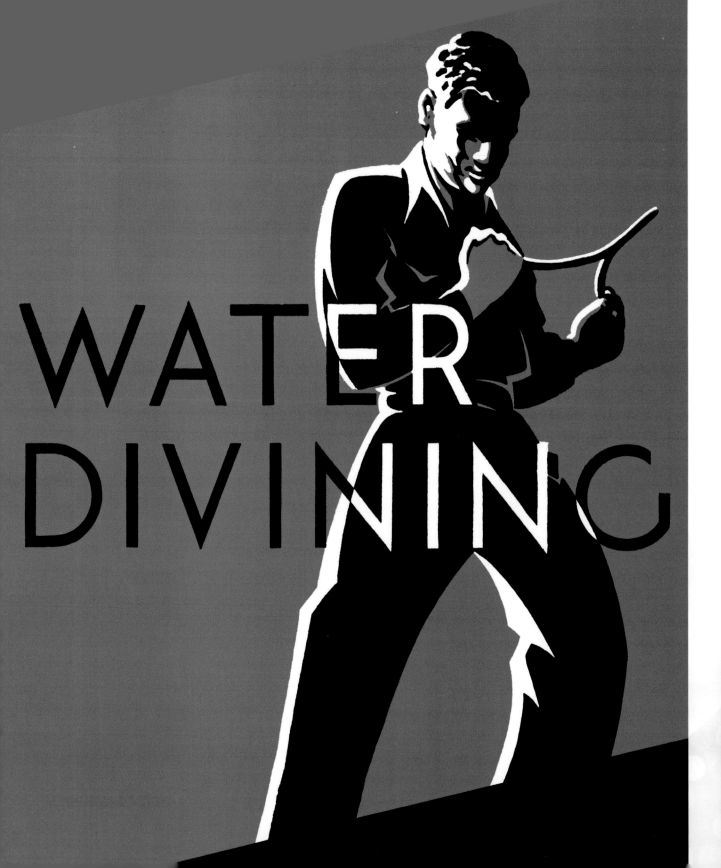

- **Abbé Alexis Mermet (1866–1937)**
  Successfully dowsed wells and located missing people.

- **Abbé Alexis-Timothée Bouly (1865–1958)**
  Was made a Chevalier de la Légion d'honneur (France's highest decoration) for his work in dowsing. Originally a water dowser, he helped locate and identify unexploded artillery shells before moving on to health dowsing.

- **Father Jean Jurion (1901–77)** Was adept at medical dowsing and often successfully treated patients when traditional doctors had failed.

'For the newcomer, a whole new world will be revealed, waiting to be explored beneath his feet. He will never look at the world with quite the same eyes again.'

PETER NAYLOR

Other Exceptional Dowsers

If we include examples of dowsers who used tools other than the pendulum, such as L-rods, Y-rods and bobbers, there have been many exceptional dowsers. Here are some of them.

- **T.C. Lethbridge (1901–71)** Became interested in dowsing in his later years and developed the 'long pendulum' technique to identify objects as well as concepts.

◐ **Kathe Bachler (b. 1923)** Dowsed 3,000 apartments and 500 cancer cases, successfully linking illness to harmful earth radiation (geopathic stress) and also linking 'problem' children to such places.

◐ **Brother James Kimpton (1925–2017)** Dowsed hundreds of wells in poor Indian villages, improving the villagers' health and wellbeing.

Dowsing Without a Tool

As dowsing is a natural skill, anyone can do it. In fact, you do not have to have a tool of any sort in order to dowse. Your body is naturally sensitive and responsive. A tool merely amplifies your body's response.

Using only your body is known as deviceless dowsing. There are at least 20 ways your body can give you an answer to a question, from whether you blink or not, to whether a muscle becomes strong or weak when tested.

It is likely that dowsing was first done without a tool and later, tools were adopted to make the process easier.

The Right Tool for the Job

The most popular dowsing tools are the L-rod, the Y-rod and the pendulum. The rods are named for their respective shapes. The Y-rod moves up and down to indicate 'yes' or 'no', and the L-rod moves from side to side.

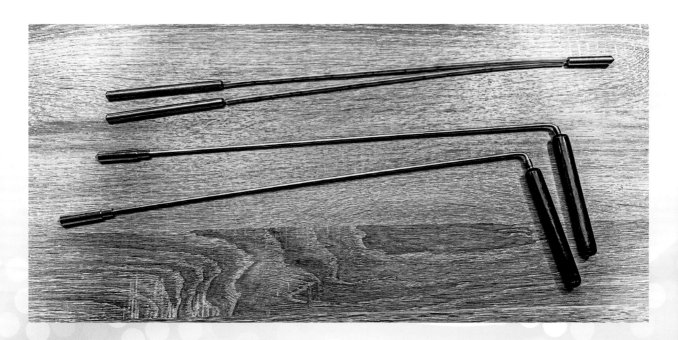

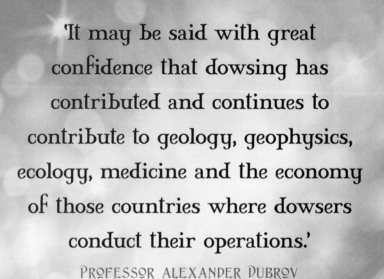

'It may be said with great confidence that dowsing has contributed and continues to contribute to geology, geophysics, ecology, medicine and the economy of those countries where dowsers conduct their operations.'

PROFESSOR ALEXANDER DUBROV

Rods are more often used outdoors, because they are less prone to making involuntary movements and will give a much more definite response than a pendulum. There is a longer recorded history of the use of rods in dowsing as opposed to pendulums, partly because, historically, dowsing mostly took place outdoors. As other applications of dowsing were added – most of them taking place indoors – the pendulum soon became the most popular dowsing tool.

pendulums can be taken anywhere and put to more discreet use than rods, so they became the tool of choice for most dowsers.

Late in the twentieth century, as vibrational medicine became popular, practitioners decided to use the energy frequency of a pendulum during healing sessions to boost results. Pendulum healing became a whole new use of pendulums.

'Dowsing has undergone a paradigm shift from the finding of water sources, lumps of metal and old drains, to the realms of a spiritual search into the mysteries of human consciousness and its relationship with the earth.'

HAMISH MILLER

The Evolution of Pendulums

Since the late nineteenth century, people have found many more uses for dowsing pendulums as they began to realize dowsing is just asking a question and getting an answer. Being lightweight and easy to carry,

HOW DO PENDULUMS WORK?

With proper technique, a pendulum can be a tool for transforming your life. Once you master technique and are getting results that please you, you may wonder what exactly is going on when you swing a pendulum. While no one is able to prove how pendulums work, there are some interesting theories.

'There is no totally convincing explanation of how dowsing works, but there is more and more evidence that it does work.'

JANE THURNELL-READ

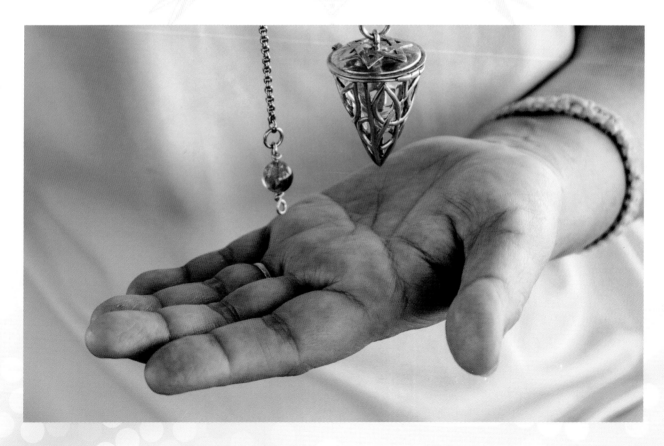

The Power Comes from Within

When you understand that a pendulum is merely a tool, it makes sense to accept that the power of the pendulum is *you*. The pendulum amplifies the answer to your dowsing question. Like a speedometer in a car, it displays information you want in a simple way, but in a sense, it is just a gauge.

The pendulum does this by amplifying your body's subtle response to the question, making it easy to see. This response is called the 'ideomotor response'. So the first lesson in pendulum dowsing is not to think of the pendulum as giving you the answers. *You* are providing the answers.

Where Do the Answers Come From?

How can you be providing answers to questions when you do not know the answer? Some people say the answers are in the Akashic Records, a sort of big spiritual library. Others attribute answers to your spirit guides or your High Self.

TIP

If you can find the answer to your question using rational means, do not waste your time dowsing about it.

We do not believe answers come from God, your spirit guides or an advanced being. That is a technique called channelling, which is when you are communicating with a spiritual being of some kind.

With dowsing, you are looking inward, not outward, and whether you are consulting a higher level of your own consciousness or you are consulting the Akashic Records, the answers are coming through you.

'If dowsers are operating by mere chance, it's pretty amazing how they can be so successful.'

AMIT GOSWAMI

What About Wrong Answers?

There is a common misconception that any so-called psychic activity is or should be accurate 100 per cent of the time. Dowsing has often been classified as a psychic gift, so sceptics will point to wrong answers as proof that dowsing does not work.

Dowsing is a natural skill, not a psychic power. As with any skill, there is a learning curve, and proper technique is necessary. Practice will improve your results in a given dowsing application to 90 per cent or higher. But even veteran dowsers sometimes get wrong answers, because no human activity is perfect.

How Does Pendulum Healing Work?

A healing pendulum has a specific shape and material that give it a unique vibrational frequency. When used in pendulum healing, the pendulum helps focus the healing energy of the practitioner. A healing pendulum is analogous to a pointed crystal used in crystal healing.

There are different styles of healing pendulums with different frequencies, just as crystals or colours have different frequencies of energy. The frequency of the pendulum, when combined with the therapist's own frequency, generates a unique vibrational frequency.

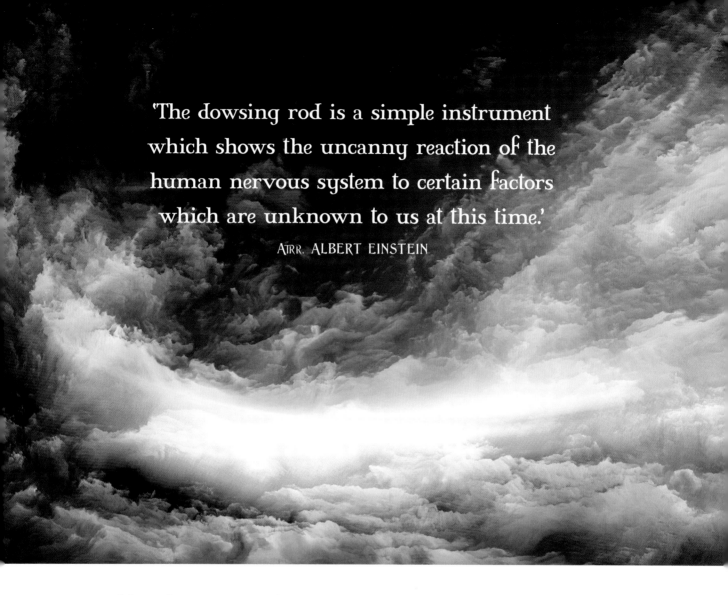

'The dowsing rod is a simple instrument which shows the uncanny reaction of the human nervous system to certain factors which are unknown to us at this time.'

ATTR. ALBERT EINSTEIN

So a given pendulum will not work the same for every healer. Thus, most pendulum healers have a variety of pendulums for different jobs.

Does Healing Always Occur?

No matter what healing method you use, conventional or natural, you do not always get the results you desire. Sometimes this is because the practitioner is not yet an expert. There is truth to the saying that 'practice makes perfect'.

Even experts do not always work miracles. Healing occurs in layers, and sometimes to get the desired results, several sessions are needed. The deeper levels heal before the obvious symptoms. Another contributing factor is that the energy of the healer and their method will work best if they resonate with the vibration of the person being treated.

CHOOSING A PENDULUM FOR DOWSING

There are no hard and fast rules about choosing a dowsing pendulum. You can make your own with available materials, or you can buy one. The important thing to remember is since the pendulum is just a tool for indicating answers, the material does not matter. You can dowse with any weighted object on a string or chain.

Make Your Own

A necklace with a pendant makes a great dowsing pendulum, especially if you wear it all the time. Just take the necklace off and dowse with it. A set of keys on a chain is another suitable everyday object. For those with a tight budget, a metal nut on a length of dental floss makes an inexpensive dowsing pendulum. If you have the skill, you can make a beautiful dowsing pendulum using beads and other jewellery supplies. We have used all of these types of pendulums, and they all work well.

> ### TIP
>
> You do not need to spend a lot of money to get a good pendulum.

Let One Choose You

It is fun to go to a New Age store that offers a selection of dowsing pendulums of different materials

'Dowsing is more than a
subject, it's a skill, a tool –
one which I suppose can be
used to tackle any problem
you care to name.'

TOM GRAVES

and designs. Most people find that if they 'try out' a variety of pendulums in a store, one (and sometimes more than one) will 'speak' to them. The right pendulum for you will often be so attractive that it seems to have chosen you. Such a pendulum is one you will value for many years.

A Different Pendulum for Each Job

Most dowsers have several pendulums and will use different ones for specific tasks. Sometimes one

design works better than others. A pointed end
will make a pendulum more useful for chart dowsing,
for example.

> 'Remember that dowsing is
> an inner process, and that
> your pendulum is simply a
> tool for discovering wisdom
> and not the source of it.'
>
> DR PATRICK MACMANAWAY

You Cannot Go Wrong

Since there are so many possible pendulum designs,
there are no wrong choices. It all comes down to
personal preference. We have found that a heavier
pendulum, such as one made of brass, has a nice
weight that makes dowsing 'feel' better than when
working with a lightweight pendulum made of wood.

> ## TIP
>
> The pendulum that most attracts you
> and feels best is the one to buy.

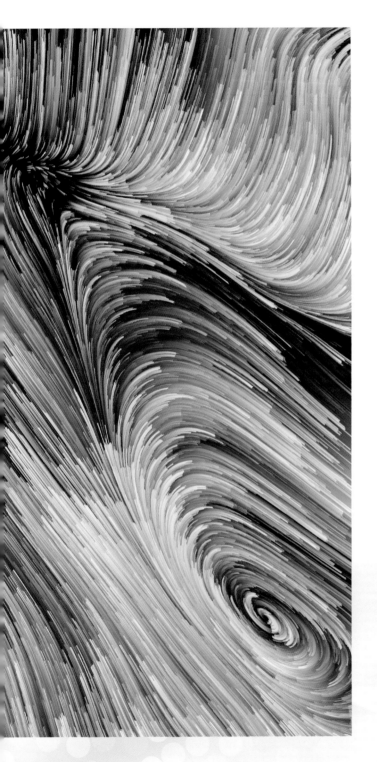

We have tried every type of pendulum you can imagine, and in the end, we have found that simple works best for us. But part of the fun is the journey. Enjoy experimenting with different pendulums and find out what works best for you.

> 'Emergency pendulums, like bath brushes with a hanging loop, key chains, nails or fat paperclips often helped me.'
>
> WALTER LÜBECK

Do Pendulums Need Maintenance?

We have heard people say you should never allow someone else to use your pendulum. Or that you need to cleanse it before each use. While it is inevitable that rituals evolve around practices like healing and dowsing, we have found that most of the time they are not needed. The only maintenance we have found necessary is for crystal pendulums, if the crystal is one that accumulates energies. Any crystal used in a pendulum should be cleared on the recommended schedule for that crystal. And it is perfectly all right to allow someone else to handle or use your pendulum.

GETTING STARTED WITH PENDULUM DOWSING

Dowsing is a natural human skill that anyone can learn. It allows you to focus your intuition to get an answer to a question your brain cannot answer. At first, you may find it takes a bit of time to go through all the steps. Be patient. You'll get faster the more often you dowse.

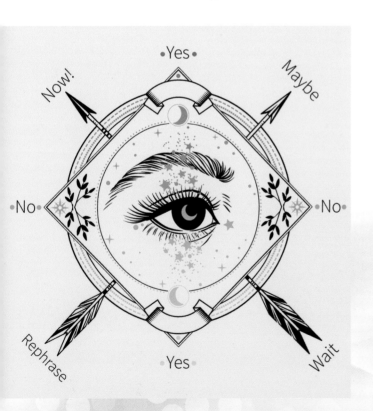

'Yes' or 'No'?

You need to know which pendulum movements are 'yes' and 'no' before you begin to ask questions. Some people use circular motions, while others prefer linear motions. Both work just fine. You can experiment and decide which is best for you. Usually, with linear motions, 'yes' is out and back like nodding your head for 'yes', while 'no' is side to side, like a negative head motion. Circular motions are clockwise and anticlockwise, with 'yes' most often being clockwise.

TIP

When learning to dowse, keep your fingers pointed downwards to allow the pendulum to swing freely.

What Is Your Yes/No Response?

You can determine your pendulum's motions a couple of different ways. One way is to 'programme' it. You

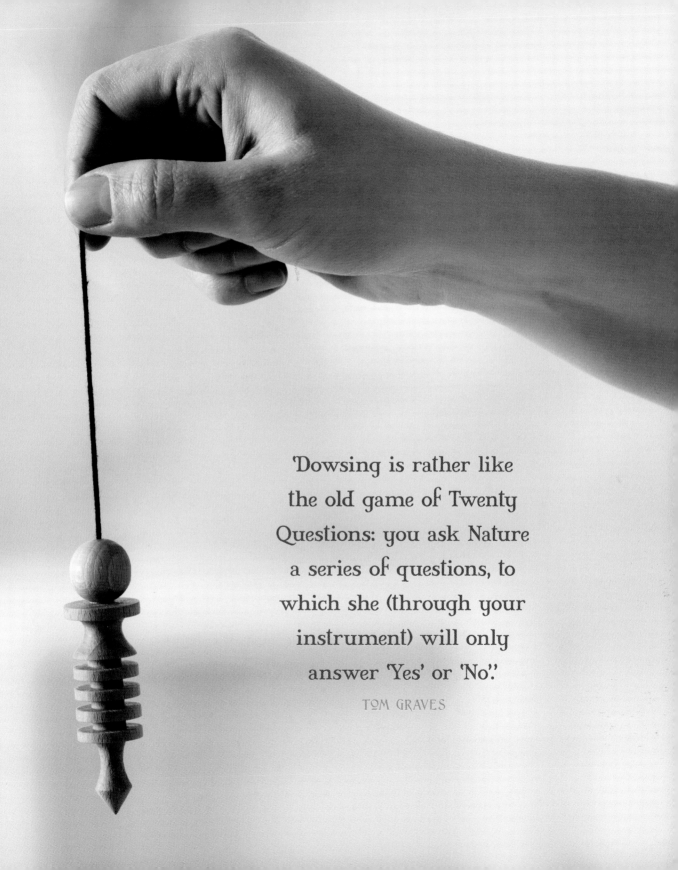

'Dowsing is rather like
the old game of Twenty
Questions: you ask Nature
a series of questions, to
which she (through your
instrument) will only
answer 'Yes' or 'No'.'

TOM GRAVES

can focus and say, 'This is my "yes"' while swinging the pendulum in your preferred 'yes' motion. Then do the same with your preferred 'no' movement.

Alternatively, you can just test what your natural responses are by asking a question you know is true. Your birthplace is a good example. To see your 'yes' response, ask 'Was I born in X?', X being the correct answer. To see your 'no' response, ask about a false location.

'Dowsing can take us into the heart of the mystery which is life itself. There is no power in the pendulum itself; the power is within us.'

NAOMI OZANIEC

41

STEP ❶: What's Your Goal?

Before you begin, take a few minutes to think about *why* you want an answer to your question. Are you asking about taking that job offer because you want to make the most money you can, or because you want the best opportunity for advancement?

Your answer will differ depending on your goal. So be clear what your goal is. It is helpful to have a dowsing journal and write this down.

TIP

Remember to have fun with dowsing.
It is not supposed to be a test.

STEP ❷: Form the Question

For best results, take the time to formulate a detailed question and write it down in your dowsing journal before you dowse, so you can check back later and measure accuracy or learn from mistakes. A good dowsing question includes how, when, where, why, what and who.

You will get better results if you avoid vague words and phrases such as 'good'. Define terms clearly. A good dowsing question is usually long.

> 'Poor questioning ability
> is actually the most
> common factor behind why
> those learning to dowse
> consequently give up.'
> ELIZABETH BROWN

STEP ❸: Get into a Dowsing State

This critical part of the process is often skipped, and the result is the person is not really dowsing. Dowsing requires a different brain state than your normal one.

The best way to think of it is as a sort of meditative state where you empty your mind of everything but the question.

Your emotional state is harmonious and one of curiosity. Detachment, curiosity, calm and focus are required for the dowsing state. Brain wave tests have shown this altered state in dowsers most closely resembles the brain activity of a powerful energy healer.

STEP ❹: Dowse

When you feel you are in a dowsing state, put your pendulum in what is called a 'neutral swing', which is neither 'yes' nor 'no' for you. Having it swing in a line at a 45-degree angle to the 'yes' is one option. The point is to give some momentum to the pendulum so that the answer can more easily be seen.

Then ask your question. If your question is terribly long and you have written it down and read it to yourself a few times beforehand and focused on it, when you do the actual dowsing, you can just ask what the answer is to your question, meaning the one you wrote down. Record your answer in your dowsing journal.

Your Learning Curve Is Unique

Over time, your dowsing yes/no answers may change, or you may get additional pendulum movements that add new answers like 'bad question', 'none of your business' or 'maybe'.

Keeping a dowsing journal will help you chart progress and see patterns that help you interpret new movements.

Another benefit of a journal is that you can go back to find out why your answer appeared to be wrong. Often, your answer is correct for the question you asked, but your question was not specific enough or lacked an important detail, like a time frame. Look at your question and analyse how your answer could be right for *that* question. Then make a better question next time.

45

EVERYDAY DOWSING

Dowsing every day is the secret to mastering dowsing. Everyday dowsing provides you with a variety of situations where you need and want an answer your brain cannot provide. Take advantage of such times to hone your skill before you proceed to more challenging applications. It is the element of need combined with emotional detachment that makes everyday dowsing such a great learning experience. Never dowse coin tosses or card suits. Dowse about something that will improve your life.

Can You Find Lost Objects?

When we made a visit to some friends, we were taken on a walking tour of their 100-acre farm through grassy fields, wooded areas and up and down hills. On returning to the house, Maggie discovered that the small metal ball that screwed on to the end of her L-rod, which she had been using to check energies, had fallen off somewhere on the walk. Using dowsing, she was able to return to the exact location in a field where it had fallen off and recovered it. Have you ever lost something that dowsing might have found?

Find Your Lost Keys (and Other Things)

If you discover your keys or an earring or your wallet is missing and you know it is located somewhere in your house, you can dowse where to find it by following these steps:

1   Your goal is to find your keys.

2   Your question can be: 'In which room of my house are my keys located at this time?'

3   Get into a dowsing state by dropping fear, being curious and focusing on the question.

4   Dowse the question, naming each room after you ask the main question. One room will give you a 'yes' response.

'Use dowsing as a way of life rather than an interesting hobby.'

DENNIS WHEATLEY

Find Your Friend's Lost Ring (and Other Things)

What if the object you wish to find is not at your present location? Maybe a friend in another town asks you to find her lost ring in her house.

Map dowsing is perfect for remote dowsing. Using a sketch of the area you want to dowse, follow the instructions in the previous section to locate where exactly the lost object is. You can point to a room or name an area on the map while dowsing.

When dowsing for lost objects, it is wise to start by first asking if the object is currently located in the building or area you are dowsing.

Dowse a Takeaway Menu

How often have you been disappointed when you ordered a meal in a restaurant or from a takeaway menu? Dowsing can help you avoid frustration by giving you answers you cannot get through rational means.

You can use it to:

- Pick an item that will be most satisfying for you.

- Avoid allergens or additives.

- Choose the most nutritious item.

- If you have multiple menus, dowse which place to order from for the fastest service.

- Dowse among menus for the one with the meal you would most enjoy that day.

You can do this same type of dowsing in a restaurant if you wish. Dowsing in public is simpler and stealthier if you use deviceless methods, so we suggest you learn one of those for public use.

Select the Best Gift

When you buy a gift for someone you love, you want them to really like it. You search and search and find what you think is the perfect gift. Unfortunately, there are often questions you have that you cannot easily answer, like:

- Does she already have one of these or one like it?

- Will she love this?

- Will she use this if I get it for her?

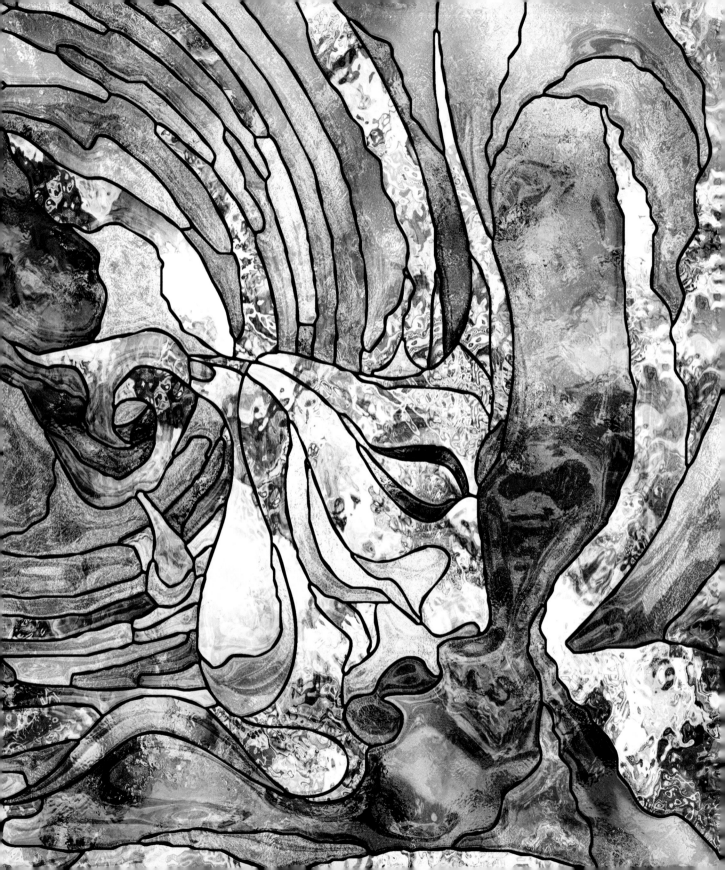

Avoid disappointment and wasted money by using dowsing to determine that the gift you have in mind will not be a duplicate, will be cherished and will be used.

Help Your Plants Thrive

Even if you have green fingers – but especially if you do not – you will find dowsing is a remarkable tool for helping your plants not only survive, but thrive.

Here are some of the more common uses:

- Select the best location inside or outside for the plant.
- Choose soil amendments and fertilizers.
- Check your watering schedule.
- Discover if the plant has a disease or infestation.
- Select the right product or method for resolving problems.

'A plant is alive. It presents a wonderful learning opportunity for you. Even a small houseplant will teach you something.'

NAOMI OZANIEC

Dowsing is not meant to replace study and research, but rational means will only take you so far, and dowsing will help you reach your gardening goals.

> ## TIP
>
> It is natural to doubt your dowsing at first. Confidence comes from practice and success, and everyday dowsing is the best way to build confidence.

Choose the Best Multivitamin

Good supplements are expensive. How do you know which brand will work best for you? How do you know whether you even *need* a multivitamin? Do not let advertising make your choice. Dowse what is best for your goals.

This is a good example of where your goals need to be clear and specific. What are you trying to accomplish by taking a supplement? Stronger immunity and fewer illnesses? More energy? A more focused mind? Better digestion?

Your question will need to take into account the recommended dosage, price, side effects and anything else that matters to you, so it will probably be very long.

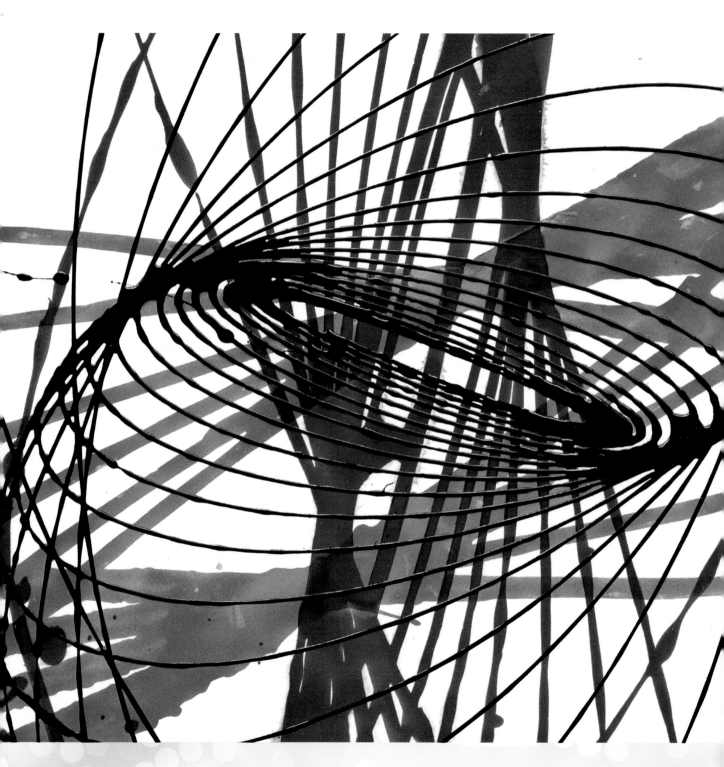

Find the Best Plumber (or Other Service Person)

When you need an accountant or roofer and you do not know whom to choose, dowsing will give you the best answer. Goals matter here and are unique to you.

You may want:

- ◐ the fastest service

- ◐ the cheapest service

- ◐ the most reliable person

- ◐ the highest-quality performance

- ◐ the best guarantee

More than likely, you want a combination of those things. Get very clear about all your goals and then dowse which among your choices will satisfy you best in general. You can also dowse the individual items on the list to see strengths and weaknesses of providers before choosing.

Boy or Girl?

You can dowse to determine if you are pregnant and, if so, whether your baby will be a boy or girl. Modern

medicine can give you answers to those questions if you want them, but this subject makes a good dowsing exercise before you buy a test, or if your friend asks you to dowse for her.

> 'Use dowsing to help you learn to watch, to observe, to see; to listen, to feel; to help you build up and use your intuition.'
>
> TOM GRAVES

This situation highlights the importance of detachment. If being pregnant would have negative consequences for you, your emotions will make it impossible to be simply curious about the answer. Do not dowse.

Make no assumptions. Maggie has first cousins who are triplets. When dowsing sex, remember there may be more than one baby.

If you desperately want a boy rather than a girl, your attachment to a certain answer will probably make you get the answer you want. If that is the case, do not dowse.

LIFE CHOICES

Even when you follow dowsing protocol carefully, sooner or later you will wish you could get more than just 'yes' or 'no' for an answer. This is especially true when making major life choices. Dowsing excels in situations where you need to make a big decision that could have major emotional, financial or physical impact in the future. But if all you can get is 'yes' or 'no', you will probably hesitate to trust your dowsing.

Beyond 'Yes' or 'No'

If you have been dowsing every day on things that will improve your life, you will gain confidence and hone your dowsing skill. Then you will want to take on bigger challenges, like choosing a house to buy or selecting the perfect career.

> '**I think it would be very foolish not to take the irrational seriously.**'
>
> JEANETTE WINTERSON

While detachment and the right question are vital at these times, having a wider range of answers is as important. Scales are a great way to get more than a 'yes' or 'no'. With scales, you get a whole range from 'heck, yeah' to 'yikes, no'.

Scales Improve Your Answers

There are many scales you can use when dowsing. You can either use a sketch of the scale (shown here) or visualize it in your head or on the table top while you dowse. See the Resources section at the end of the book for more on scales and charts.

The 0 to 10 scale can be a simple line marked with the numbers 0 to 10 evenly spaced. This simple scale conveys a degree of 'yes' or 'no' as well as showing levels of effects of a given choice.

The -10 to +10 scale looks like a protractor with 0 at the top of the curve and the -10 and +10 on opposite

Dowsing Charts Scales

Numbered scales can be based on either 0 to 10 or -10 to +10, depending on what you prefer

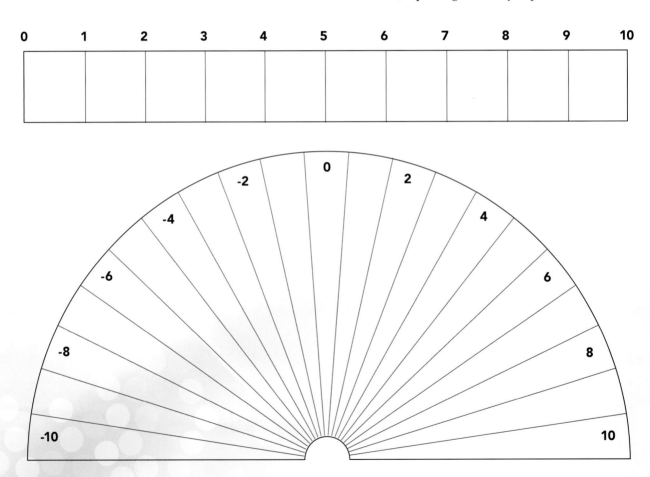

ends of the horizontal. It is great for showing positive, negative and neutral effects in varying degrees.

How to Use Scales

The 0 to 10 scale is easiest to use, because you can say the numbers slowly after asking your question and note which number gives you the 'yes' response with your pendulum.

The -10 to +10 scale can be used the same way by saying the question and asking if the answer is negative, neutral, or positive in turn until you get a 'yes', then going through the numbers as needed until you find the precise answer.

An example of a dowsing question that uses scales is, 'On a scale of 0 to 10, with 8 or higher meaning I would be very satisfied, what would the result be for my goals if I took this job?'

Financial Decisions

You can use pendulum dowsing with scales to help make your investments successful. Knowing your goals and being thorough about them is important, and having positive energy about money in general aids in detachment so you can get accurate answers.

'When you reach the end of what you should know, you will be at the beginning of what you should sense.'

KAHLIL GIBRAN

When you are dowsing about an important life choice, it is vital not to let your emotions, peer pressure or enthusiasm sweep away detachment. If you have already decided you want to invest in that scheme of Uncle Jim's, your dowsing answer will not be accurate. Be honest with yourself. If you cannot be detached, do not dowse.

'The head thinks.
The heart knows.'
RASHEED OGUNLARU

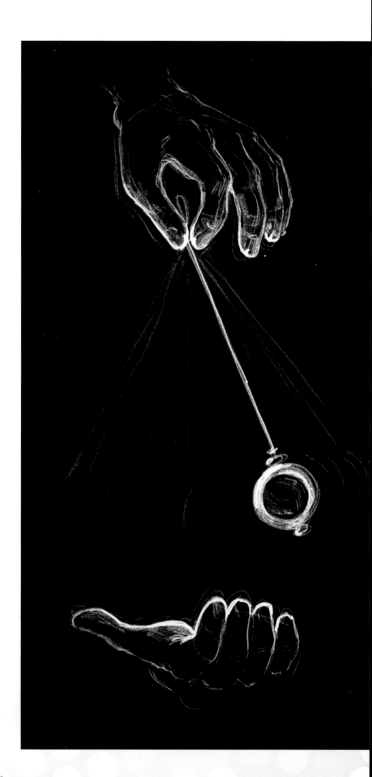

Buying a Car

Your goals for buying a car may include price, reliability, your purpose for owning a car and how soon you intend to replace it, among other things. After you list all your goals, you can form a good dowsing question that uses scales to test the value of a car you are considering.

A sample dowsing question is, 'On a scale of 0 to 10, with 8 or higher meaning I would be very pleased overall with my choice after a year of owning it, how does this car rate overall?' We use 8 as the cut-off point for taking action. If you get less, do not buy that car.

> ### TIP
>
> If you always get the answer you expect, you probably are not dowsing. Your answer should sometimes surprise you, not simply reinforce what your mind thinks or wants.

Purchasing a House

Something you will discover if you use dowsing a lot is that your intuition in general will improve. Often, the answer will come to you before you finish asking your question.

We spent a lot of time making lists of goals and working to become detached when looking for a house to buy. After months of research and preparation, we viewed three homes. When we walked into the second one, we just 'knew' it was ours. We did not have to dowse. That level of intuitive sensing seems magical, but it is a natural consequence of dowsing a lot.

> 'If we are to understand and apply dowsing in our lives, we have to expand our vision of the world we live in.'
>
> NAOMI OZANIEC

Career Choice

When you dowse about taking a job, the tricky bit is to follow through on your dowsing. Having a dowsing buddy who will confirm or deny your results can help you build trust in your dowsing. Your dowsing buddy should be proficient in basic dowsing technique.

At first you may doubt your answers and be afraid to follow through, so get support and use methods that build trust. Remember that your dowsing journal is a great way to chart progress.

RELATIONSHIP DOWSING

Dowsing is not meant to be used in place of communicating or using your head, but there are times when you would like some input on the direction to take in a relationship that you cannot get in a rational way. As with all dowsing, you start with your goals, because your answers will depend on what your aim is.

How to Bypass Emotions

One way to distance yourself emotionally is to use a technique called blind dowsing. Cut up pieces of paper the same size and write one of the possible answers on each piece; if you only want a yes/no answer, do three 'yes' and three 'no' papers. Fold them up identically. Mix them in a bowl and toss them on the floor or a table.

Get into a dowsing state and ask your question after putting your pendulum into a neutral swing. Say, 'Give me a "yes" when I point at the best answer.' Alternatively, pick up each paper and ask, 'Is this the best answer?' Stop dowsing after your first 'yes' answer.

Choose an Animal Companion

Compatibility is the key to success in any relationship, and dowsing is an excellent way to determine it. When choosing a pet, make a list of the things that are important for a happy pet relationship for you.

Follow the steps for dowsing, using the question, 'How compatible in general on a scale of 0 to 10 is this animal for my goals, with 8 or higher meaning we will

'The spirit of self
has a small, still voice.
One of the ways that
we can learn to listen
closely to it is by
learning how to dowse.'

DR PATRICK MACMANAWAY

have a long-term happy relationship?' You can dowse individual aspects of compatibility as well. Do not adopt or buy an animal if the number is less than 8.

Talk to Animals

A little-known application of dowsing is basic animal communication. If you are proficient with basic dowsing technique, you can use yes/no questions to ask about or to directly make inquiries of your animal companion.

Wouldn't it be nice to be sure your pet wants to participate in that obedience class? Or would like to have a furry sister or brother? You can use dowsing to fine-tune your pet's diet, identify behavioural problems and their causes, and select training or breeding programmes. Dowsing is a great way to strengthen the human-animal connection.

Love

In the year 2000, the authors of this book met online at a dowsing forum. Nigel was in the UK, Maggie was in Arizona in the US. After they exchanged a few emails about dowsing, Maggie had an intuitive feeling that Nigel was meant to be someone special in her life.

Having recently learned to dowse, Maggie decided to apply this skill to find out what role Nigel was meant to fulfill in her life: friend, dowsing buddy, dowsing mentor, lover or life partner. When the answer was life partner, Maggie had a big choice to make. She quit her job, stored her belongings and set out for the UK to meet Nigel.

Without dowsing, Maggie would probably not have had the courage to follow through on such a big change without a guarantee of success. But thanks to dowsing, she found her life partner. The rest, as they say, is history.

> ## TIP
>
> The answer you get, even a 'wrong' answer, is often a correct answer for the question you asked.

Partnership and Friendship

Choosing a friend or selecting a business partner is just as important as finding your soulmate. The focused intuition of dowsing can give you a compatibility number that confirms or denies your feelings.

'Dowsing enables us to explore the strange world of matter, energy and consciousness.'
NAOMI OZANIEC

As with most intuitive techniques concerning relationships, you must put aside your emotions for best results. Infatuation can skew your results in love relationships, while enthusiasm, hope and even other people's desires can lead you astray in business and other personal situations.

Taking action can be a real challenge in life-changing situations, and dowsing can give you the extra courage you need to do what is best for you.

TIP

Following through on your dowsing answer can be hard, so practise doing that on simpler subjects first to build your confidence in your dowsing.

Marriage

Dowsing will help you avoid marrying someone who isn't right for you. One technique you can use for this is to ask how you would feel about the marriage at a future time, for example, in four years.

> ## 'The answers you get are only as good as the questions you ask.'
> MAGGIE PERCY

This is a specific example of future dowsing that actually tends to be accurate if you have mastered basic dowsing technique. Put aside your fear and ask,

'If I marry X, how will I feel about that decision four years from now on a 0 to 10 scale, with 8 or higher meaning I will be happy I married him/her?'

Divorce

Dissolving a marriage is not lightly done, and dowsing can give you the extra confidence you need to decide if your marriage can be saved or not. It can also help you to know the side effects of choosing divorce.

You can use the -10 to +10 scale and ask, 'On a scale of -10 to +10, with negative numbers meaning bad outcomes, what will be the overall long-term effect on my life if I divorce X?'

Using the same scale, you can determine the effects on your finances in a given time period, on the children and on your health and wellbeing.

76

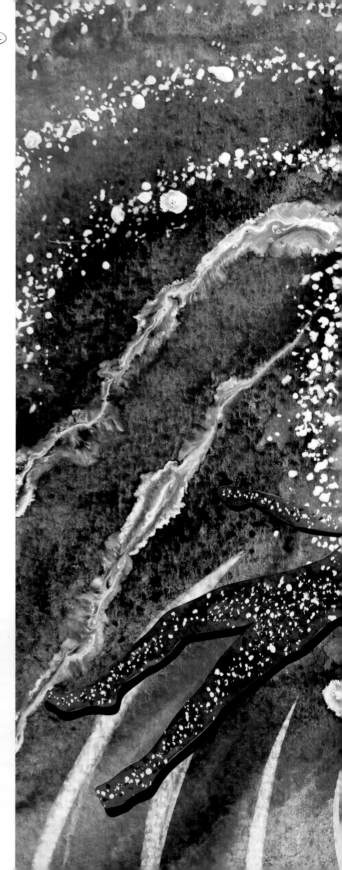

HEALTH DOWSING

Dowsing for health is probably the most popular dowsing application, yet few dowsers ever go beyond dowsing their supplements. This is because health dowsing is complex compared to other applications and requires a basic understanding of human biology as well as masterful technique. In this section, we'll share some priceless techniques and applications anyone can learn.

Caution

No human endeavour is perfect. When dowsing about health, please get a second and even a third opinion before taking action. You can use dowsing to help you select your health professional or healing team. Always consult a professional when appropriate.

Lists and Charts

Often when dowsing for health, you are selecting from a vast array of possible choices. Lists and charts allow you to dowse the best among many options.

'Dowsing can be used in preventative as well as curative medicine. This is one of the most valuable uses of medical dowsing – for surely prevention is better than cure?'

TOM GRAVES

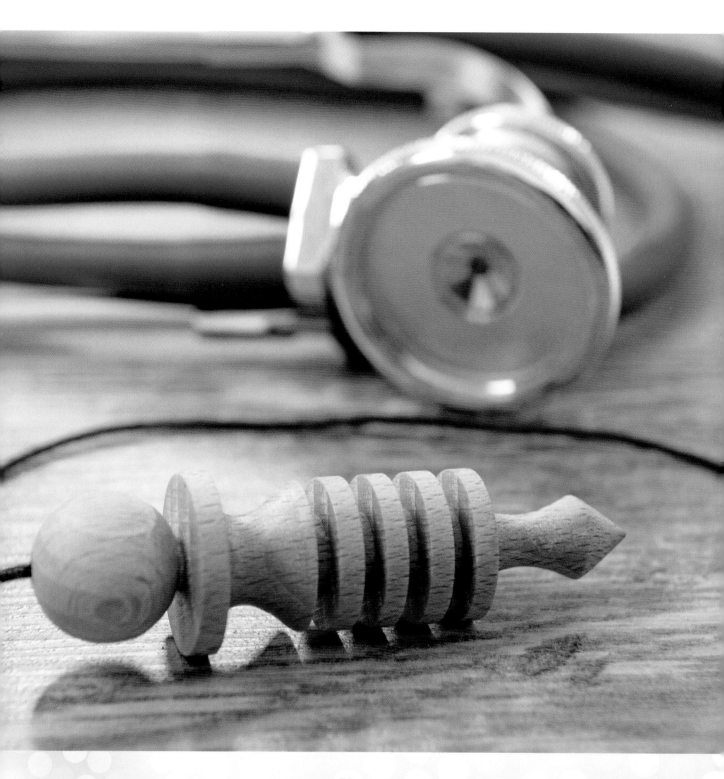

A list or chart should always include 'other' as a choice in case the list is incomplete. Use a chart as you would a scale. Get your tool into a neutral swing, then ask your question. If using a chart, let the pendulum settle to swinging over the answer. With a list, point to or say each option until you get a 'yes' response.

Programming a Question

It is expedient to 'programme' certain questions in advance so you can use a short form and dowse in an emergency. Preparing in advance means you consider all aspects of your goal and decide under what conditions you want a 'yes' or 'no'. For example, a pet health emergency might include your budgetary limits, whether you have the ability to solve the problem yourself, or if a professional would be able to resolve it quicker or better.

'In order to heal themselves, people must recognize, first, that they have an inner guidance deep within and, second, that they can trust it.'

SHAKTI GAWAIN

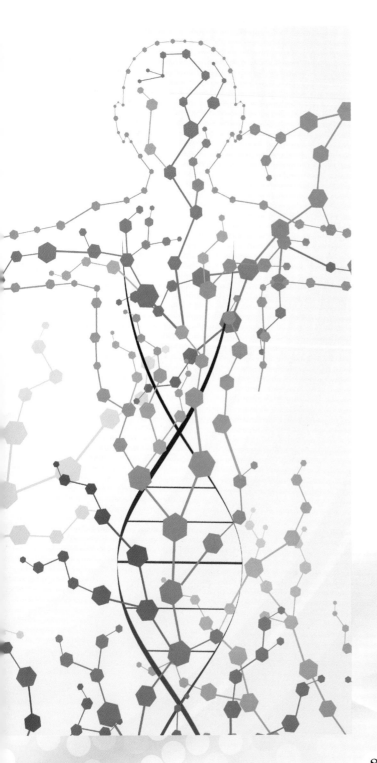

Make your dowsing question and write it down in your journal. Select a short form that will represent the long question and set your intention that whenever you ask that short question, you get a dowsing answer for the longer question. Doing this will improve your accuracy at a time when you are under a lot of stress.

> 'Allopathic doctors used to laugh condescendingly at those who posited that psychological, emotional and spiritual factors were important contributors to the sickness as well as healing of the body.'
>
> MARIANNE WILLIAMSON

Good or Bad?

If you have recently started an exercise programme, new supplement or a detox, you may get unpleasant symptoms. You feel bad right now, but in the long run, those symptoms indicate your body is healing, strengthening or detoxing.

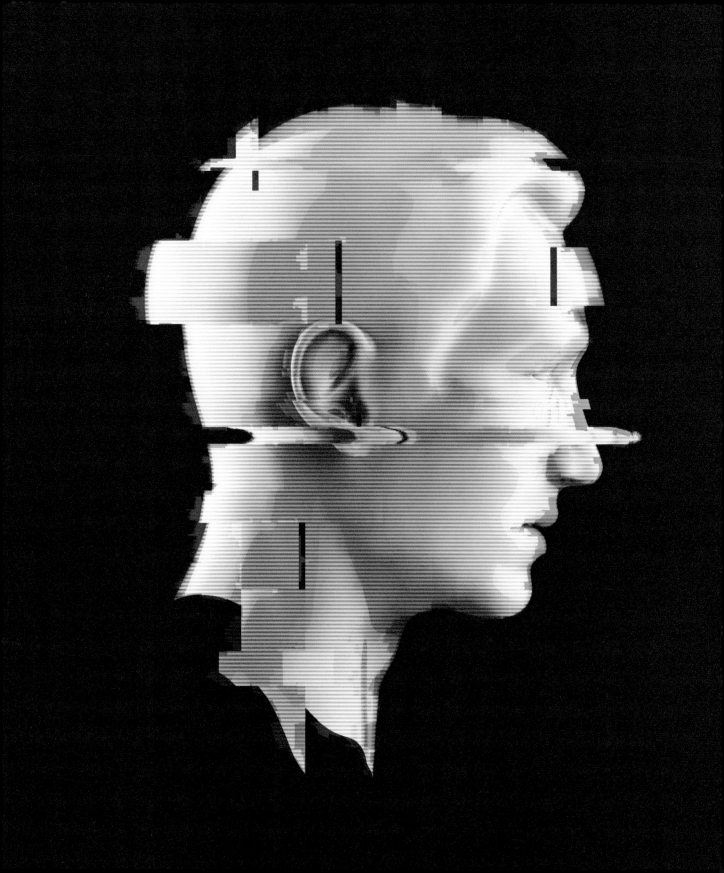

You do not want to stop a good process. Dowsing will let you know the long-term effects of any symptom so you can act appropriately.

Here is the question we use: 'On a -10 to +10 scale, with negative numbers being bad outcomes, what is the long-term level in effects on my health and wellbeing of the *cause* of this symptom?'

Measuring Side-Effects

You want to avoid anything that will do more harm than good, and since you are unique, it is hard to predict whether the drug, remedy or surgery suggested is going to have negative side-effects.

Dowsing will help you avoid unpleasant side-effects. You can use any scale you like. We use the 0 to 10 scale, with anything over 3 meaning the side-effects will be noticeable and unpleasant. You probably should not do anything that has 8 or higher negative side-effects.

Allergies and Sensitivities

A client once consulted Maggie about clearing the energy of a seafood allergy, because we have found that past lives (*see* page 113) often have a connection to strong allergies and can usually be cleared fairly easily. Maggie dowsed details of a few past lives that were involved and cleared them using intention. The client

went out and ate food that would have given him a strong reaction, and his reaction was mild. Further investigation showed that he should have asked to clear 'shellfish' allergy energy rather than just 'seafood' allergy energy. When that was cleared, he found he had no further reaction to eating shellfish.

Do I Need a Vet/Doctor?

You know when you need to go to the hospital and when you only need an over-the-counter remedy. But what about the in-between situations? Have you ever spent £300 on the vet and wondered if you really needed to go? Dowsing will save you a *lot* of money.

Programme your prepared, long emergency question using the various goals and restrictions, so that a short version such as, 'Do I need a vet?' means the same thing. When you have a critical situation is not the time to sit down, figure out goals and make a good dowsing question.

Health Is Dynamic

Everything changes, yet too often, people start a supplement or remedy and do not think to dowse whether they still need it at a later time. Something that dowses as great now may be neutral or even negative in a month or more. So use a dowsing journal and check any programme about once a month to fine-tune it.

PENDULUM HEALING

There are many energy healing modalities, but one thing they all acknowledge is that everyone has the ability to be a channel for healing energy, and that you can send that energy to another person or use it for yourself. Pendulum healing is a fairly new method that uses the vibrational frequency of a pendulum to boost the healer's ability to channel and direct healing energy.

Intention Does It All

All energy healing and transformation techniques operate through intention. Lynne McTaggart showed in her book *The Intention Experiment* that groups of people have the power to heal and transform even past events. But an individual usually requires training to be able to get into the altered brain state of a successful healer, because focusing intention is a skill.

PENDULUM HEALING

Interestingly, that brain state is similar to the brain pattern of a dowser while in the dowsing state. Therefore, being an accomplished dowser gives you an advantage in pendulum healing.

'Healing,' Papa would tell me, 'is not a science, but the intuitive art of wooing nature.'

W.H. AUDEN

91

Choosing a Pendulum for Healing

The pendulum is a tool for helping the pendulum healer focus and send healing energy. Other healing modalities use crystals or symbols (as in reiki).

The size, shape and material of a pendulum will affect its vibrational frequency. The goal is to pick one or more pendulums that resonate with your frequency and help you to power your intention. Be clear about your goal and select a pendulum that 'feels' right, then work with it.

You may find different pendulums work better for different jobs. You are unique, so follow your intuition to pick the best tool for you.

'You and I are all as much continuous with the physical universe as a wave is continuous with the ocean.'

ALAN WATTS

It Is Simple

The steps in pendulum healing are similar to dowsing. The pendulum healer has a goal, focuses on that goal

with a detached attitude and then makes a command or statement of the desired outcome.

That command should have no negative words, but rather should state the desired goal. Do not say, 'Stop this pain.' Say something like, 'Restore comfort and harmony to all levels, physical, emotional and spiritual.' Always focus on what you want, not what you do not want.

> ## 'It's when we start working together that the real healing takes place.'
> DAVID HUME

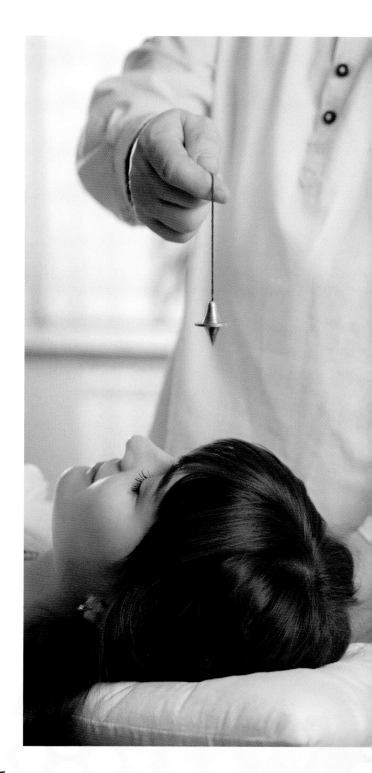

Swing the pendulum while making your command and stay focused on your command with detachment until the swinging stops. Success will depend mainly on your clarity of thought, your detachment and your ability to focus your intention.

Work in Person and Remotely

As with any modality, pendulum healing works just as well remotely as in person. Intention operates over both spatial and temporal distances, meaning it is possible to use intention to heal a past situation or a condition taking place on the other side of the globe.

Quantum mechanics makes it possible to explain why this works, but the simplest way of explaining it is that all things are connected, and you can use that connection to affect just about anything, anytime, anywhere ... *if* you can power your intention.

Get Permission

Ethical healing practices of all kinds acknowledge the free will of the participant and provide informed consent, allowing the client to accept or reject help. Even if your intention is good, you still need permission before working on another person. Always ask before doing a healing session for someone.

Not only is it unethical to work on someone without permission, it is impractical. This is a free-will universe, and although it is possible to affect someone else briefly with your intention, ultimately, they get to choose their path. Thus, work done without permission rarely has a lasting influence.

What If Nothing Happens?

Just because you do not see instant change does not mean the healing session failed. Healing is a complex process and, in general, a long-standing condition will take longer to heal and go through more 'layers' of healing (require more sessions) than a more recent condition.

There are many factors that impact success when it comes to healing. All methods work, but they do not work equally well for every person and situation. Most important is that the energy between the healer and client resonates with a common goal, and that the modality being used resonates with the client in a positive way.

THE SUBTLE ENERGY BODY

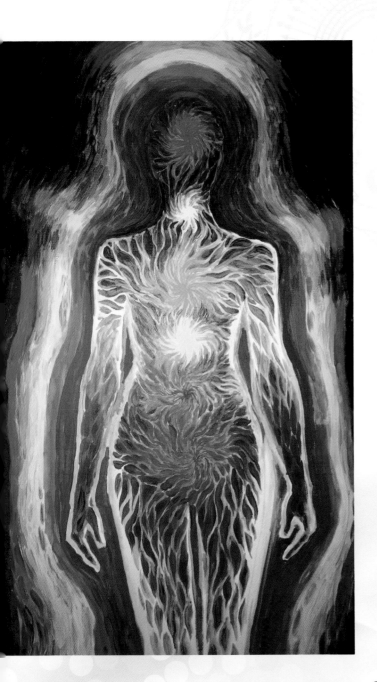

We are more than simply physical beings. We have an energetic aspect as well. This energetic aspect is constantly shifting in response to what we are doing or thinking, as well as to the environment and to other people. Think of how people and places affect you energetically. This invisible aspect of ourselves is called the subtle energy body, and we can use dowsing to explore it.

'You are the universe, you aren't in the universe.'

ECKHART TOLLE

Disease Starts Here

The easiest way of thinking about your subtle energy body is to consider it as the template and software for your physical body. Your aura surrounds you, protecting and directing your physical being. The chakras are interconnected with your body and are the channels through which energy flows through and within you. They change and react to how you live and act.

Your physical body's health depends, therefore, upon your energetic body's health. The aura should be intact and healthy, and the chakras should not be restricted or blocked.

The Aura: A Template for Health

A healthy aura has no tears or holes which compromise your physical health. Aura damage can be identified with dowsing. Nigel first realized this when dowsing over his sleeping cat and finding the energetic hole in the aura where she had been spayed.

> 'The aura given out by a person or object is as much a part of them as their flesh.'
>
> LUCIAN FREUD

You can use a pendulum to locate aura damage. By asking questions, you can discover the type of damage. You can also use it to explore the aura in as much detail as you want because it is made of seven layers. Each layer is associated with a chakra.

Identify Aura Damage

There are some people who can see a person's aura and assess its health. But the easiest way to identify aura damage is to dowse using a sketch or outline of the human body.

After first checking if there is damage, check where the worst is (front, back, left or right) and then use a pointer like a pencil to scan the area, asking for a 'yes' response from your pendulum when you have located it. Remember, the aura extends away from the body, so damage could be close in or further away.

Find a Remedy

Once located (and remember there may be more than one area that needs attention), you can then dowse to find a remedy for each location. You cannot put a plaster on something you cannot see, but there are other ways of healing.

'The whole universe appears as a dynamic web of inseparable energy patterns.... Thus we are not separated parts of a whole. We are a Whole.'

BARBARA ANN BRENNAN

Each person is different, so there is no one method for all. Amongst the most popular methods is the use

of colour or crystals. Pendulum healing is another option. Dowse to find which method will work best for each location, and then dowse which colour or crystal is best (or use pendulum healing).

Chakras: Wheels of Energy

There are seven major chakras in the body. Each major chakra is associated with a specific area and organ of the body.

The chakras are usually thought of as being wheels or vortices, in that they spin. This spinning allows the energy that animates us, sometimes called *prana* (Sanskrit) or *qi* (Chinese), to flow through us.

Too much or too little energy affects our health. A blocked chakra can lead to organ dysfunction. Optimizing the energy flow re-establishes balance and harmony in the body. Therefore, checking your chakras is important.

Check Your Chakras

The major chakras run down the midline of your body, front and back. You can check their function using dowsing.

The easiest method is to use a chart or list of the chakras. Holding your pendulum and pointing in turn at each chakra, you can ask to be shown how that chakra is functioning. Your pendulum will respond by visually representing the movement of the chakra. The direction of spin and whether it is a circle, ellipse or other form will be made clear. Do not expect consistency, as chakras are dynamic by nature.

Restore Function

Because chakras are ever-changing, you should dowse whether one is functioning properly and not make assumptions. For example, the solar plexus chakra will be sluggish after a meal.

If you dowse that a chakra is not functioning correctly, then use your pendulum to discover how best to rectify it.

Each chakra has a colour associated with it. It might be that the energy of a specific colour, delivered in some form, such as a crystal, wearing or holding an item of that colour, carrying a piece of paper of that colour, or even looking at that colour for a period of time, is required to restore the chakra. Colours are proven to affect behaviour and emotion.

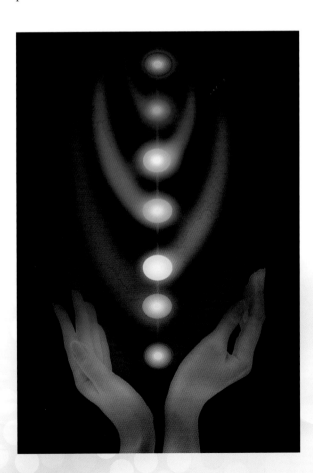

Check the effectiveness of pendulum healing. You can also use intention. Focus on restoring the chakra to its optimal function. Dowse for completion.

> 'If all the information of the cosmos flows through our pores at every moment, then our current notion of our human potential is only a glimmer of what it should be.'
>
> LYNNE MCTAGGART

Once Is Not Enough

Checking and repairing once is not enough. Your aura and chakras constantly respond to you, your thoughts and the environment. Regular checking and repair are beneficial. If one chakra always requires attention, find out to which aspect of the body it relates and research ways to fortify it.

The subtle aspects of the body have long been known about. Much has been discovered and written. The aura, for example, has many layers and there are many other chakras. You can dive deeply into exploring your non-physical body. Dowsing is the best tool for this.

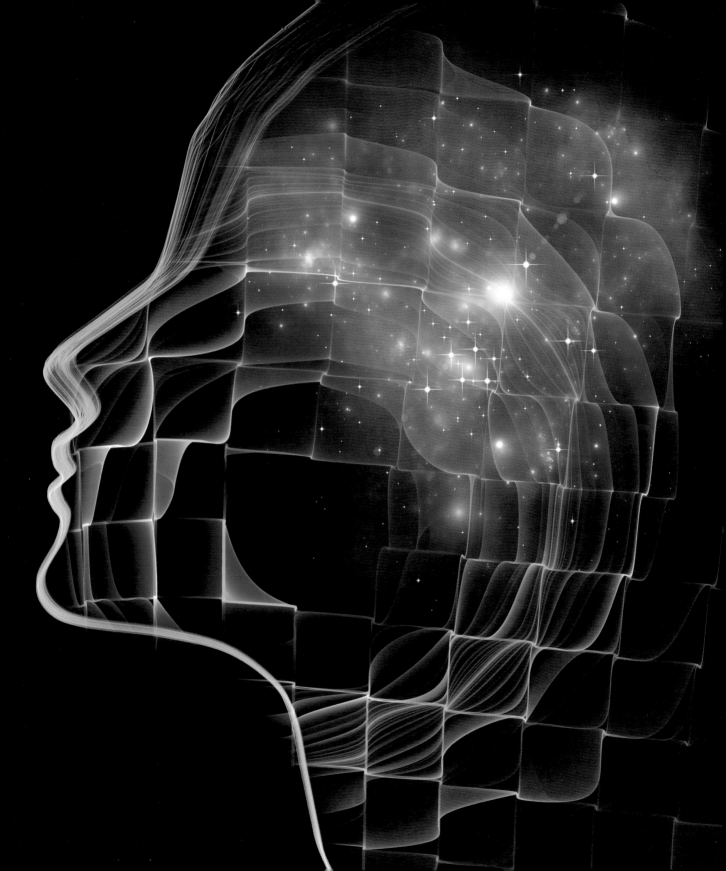

UNSEEN INFLUENCES

What you cannot see can either harm or help you. Not all unseen or energetic influences are harmful, but the detrimental ones are the ones you most want to be aware of, as they can affect your health, relationships and finances. Dowsing, as focused intuition, is the best way to gather information about the unseen influences that can affect your life, as well as to pick the best way to resolve them.

Invisible Influences Are Many

Negative external unseen influences vary from noxious environmental energies to curses and ghosts. Detrimental internal influences are many and include faulty subconscious beliefs and past-life connections and influences.

All of these mechanisms are very hard to identify if you cannot dowse, unless you have some psychic, supersensory ability. As a dowser, you will be able to identify, measure and resolve problems such as these.

> 'Who looks outside, dreams; who looks inside, awakes.'
>
> CARL JUNG

Geopathic Stress

It has long been known that energies emanate from the earth, and that some places are conducive to human health, while others are noxious. Geopathic stress is the name for energies that are detrimental to human health, and studies have shown such energies can cause cancer and other diseases.

Different species react differently to various earth energies, so when caring for pets and plants, be aware that their reactions may differ from yours. Dowsing is the best way to identify zones of noxious energies for a given species and to choose a way of harmonizing it. Since energy is always shifting, it is recommended to check your space regularly.

> 'Even though the body appears to be material, it is not. In the deeper reality, your body is a field of energy, transformation and intelligence.'
>
> DEEPAK CHOPRA

Ghosts

Human discarnates, called ghosts, are misplaced beings that can have ill effects on the health of people and pets, as well as contribute to discord in the home or workplace.

In working with clients, we have seen wild children calm down and do their homework after being cleared of attached entities. Another client related that her

'Do you remember how electrical currents and "unseen waves" were laughed at? The knowledge about man is still in its infancy.'

ATTR. ALBERT EINSTEIN

horse, a rescue animal on which she had lavished supplements, good food and special care with no visible results, became incredibly relaxed and biddable after we removed attached entities.

Dowsing can tell you if someone has entities attached, and you can use a simple statement of intention to send that being to its right and perfect place.

Subconscious Beliefs

Science is only now beginning to explore how beliefs affect one's reality, but it is becoming clearer that much of what you experience stems from how you look at the world. The important thing to understand is that it is not so much what your conscious mind believes but what your subconscious mind believes that drives your life experience.

Since the subconscious cannot be consciously known, dowsing is the most effective way to identify what your subconscious believes. It is amazing how many subconscious beliefs conflict with our conscious goals and desires. Once identified with dowsing, those beliefs can be cleared using intention or other methods.

Past Lives

Trauma in one or more past lives can affect you in the present financially, physically and emotionally.

Unexpected or sudden death in a past life is usually the trigger.

Using dowsing, you can ask if any past lives are significantly contributing to a given allergy or condition you are experiencing. If you get 'yes', ask if you need to know the details in order to clear the energy. If not, clear using whatever energy clearing method works.

If you need to dowse details, go through a series of questions to gather data on that life and then clear it and disconnect energetically from it.

Fear Is the Enemy

Ignorance is not bliss, but simply being aware there is something scary 'out there' can lead to fear, which does more harm than good. Awareness is only the first step to living an empowered, more fulfilling and happier life.

If you are aware that there are negative unseen influences, and if you empower yourself through dowsing, you have nothing to fear. You can be confident that you are able to be aware of and respond appropriately to whatever you encounter. The only limiting factor is your dowsing skill, and that can be improved with training and practice.

VISIONS OF THE FUTURE

Dowsing the future is a form of divination like tarot or runes. While it is fun and entertaining, there are many pitfalls to attempting to predict future events. We have found that future dowsing usually is not accurate and thus tends to discourage people from believing in dowsing. So we urge people to avoid dowsing the future except under certain conditions.

What Is Time?

The human perception of time is that it is unfolding in a linear fashion, but in reality physics has shown that all time is *now*. Unfortunately, that view of time is not helpful for living life, so most humans ignore the fact that time is not what they think.

The important factor from a dowsing perspective is that how you look at time affects your dowsing results. If you believe the future has not happened, then the belief that you cannot know the future will skew your results. Likewise, a linear model of time makes you see the past as unchangeable.

> ## TIP
>
> Dowsing is a gateway
> to enhanced intuition.

'In some sense man is a microcosm of the universe; therefore what man is, is a clue to the universe. We are enfolded in the universe.'

DAVID BOHM

Can You Dowse the Future?

We all want to know the future and dowsing is an addictive way of gathering information, so if you learn to dowse, you are going to want to dowse the future. Never mind that your answers might be wrong. You tell yourself that you know the truth is out there and you need to know it.

Being aware of pitfalls will help you avoid the traps people fall into whenever they use any divination technique, including dowsing. We recommend you do not dowse the future, but if you do, there are some guidelines that will minimize errors.

Fear-Based Dowsing Does Not Work

The biggest problem with dowsing the future is that almost every time you want to do it, you are doing it from fear. You want to know the answer to reassure yourself or to try to maintain control, and so you ask what is going to happen.

Fear prevents you from having the level of detachment required for accurate dowsing. Any time you want to dowse the future, ask yourself what are you afraid is going to happen? Be honest about why you want to have control by knowing outcomes. Whenever you have fear about a subject, do not dowse.

Different Concepts = Different Answers

Even if you are not fearful, your unique perspective on time will have an effect on your answer. If you feel the future has not happened, you will tend to disbelieve you can really know what will happen.

> 'The cosmos is also within us. We're made of star-stuff. We are a way for the cosmos to know itself.'
>
> CARL SAGAN

You may believe there are parallel realities branching on your path and that a choice propels you down one branch versus another. You perhaps believe that free will means the future has not happened and you can choose differently for a different outcome.

It is beyond the scope of this book to examine the many different theories, but just be aware that your viewpoint does affect your dowsing answers.

Why Dowse the Future?

Is there any time you will benefit from dowsing the future? We have found one situation where dowsing answers are reliable. When making a choice, especially a major life decision, we have found it useful to include a future time factor in our question.

If you are buying a car or thinking of taking a job or investing a lot of money, you can ask how happy you will be in five years (or whatever length of time you wish) if you make a certain choice. As long as you are detached, you will probably get a correct answer.

A Path to Enlightenment

In order to master dowsing or pendulum healing, you learn to set goals, to focus your intention, to release fear and trust the universe. These same skills have the unexpected benefit of making you a more enlightened person.

If you desire to follow a spiritual path, to enhance your intuition and to improve your life and help those you love, the pendulum is an excellent tool that will not let you down. Whether you use it for guidance or healing, the pendulum can be your ticket to a more empowered, fulfilling life.

RESOURCES

Below are our favourite picks for the beginning dowser and pendulum healer.

Books

101 Amazing Things You Can Do with Dowsing by Maggie and Nigel Percy
This is the perfect introduction to the range of possibilities dowsing offers. With this book, you will never be lost for ways to use dowsing. Get the digital version for free at all major online booksellers.

Ask the Right Question by Maggie and Nigel Percy
With lots of ready-made dowsing questions on a variety of topics, this book helps you learn how to form your own, thus addressing the biggest challenge facing most beginners.

Dowsing for Health by Patrick MacManaway
Beautifully written and illustrated, this takes you through the basics and into areas you would not have thought about. It covers all aspects of health in sufficient detail to ensure you do not get lost.

Dowsing for Beginners by Naomi Ozaniec
A superb introduction to dowsing, easy to read and full of wonderful snippets that encourage you to go further. We keep going back to it for ideas.

The Divining Hand by Christopher Bird
The single best book on the history of dowsing. Comprehensive and well illustrated, it discusses theories and research in easily understood terms and is an excellent reference.

Hands of Light by Barbara Brennan
A wonderfully detailed guide to the subtle energy body and how you can explore it with your pendulum.

Organizations

Your country's dowsing society is the best place to discover events and local chapter meetings.

American Society of Dowsers may be found at www.dowsers.org and serves dowsers in the United States.

British Society of Dowsers is at www.britishdowsers.org and is the place for United Kingdom dowsers.

Canadian Society of Dowsers supports dowsers in Canada and their website is www.canadiandowsers.org

Websites

www.discoveringdowsing.com offers plenty of free training and the Discovering Dowsing course for a reasonable price, which includes mentoring by Maggie and Nigel.

www.pendulumalchemy.com is a website focused entirely on pendulum healing. There you will find courses and pendulums for sale.

www.mirrorwaters.com is the best place for dowsing charts. Whatever you can think of, there is probably a chart for it here.

Courses and Training

www.discoveringdowsing.com provides plenty of free dowsing training and also offers the Discovering Dowsing course on discs and USB flash/thumb drives for a reasonable price.

www.pendulumalchemy.com offers a free introductory course and paid advanced courses for pendulum healers.

SCALES & CHARTS

Scales and charts may be used in dowsing to give more useful information than a simple 'yes' or 'no'. When using a 0–10 scale or chart, you may use the numbers to indicate an intensity of 'yes' or 'no', a degree of accuracy/truth, or a per cent. The -10 to +10 scale or chart is useful when you want to discover how strongly noxious or beneficial an energy, therapy or choice would be for your goals. You may prefer circular or linear charts, depending on whether your neutral swing before dowsing is a circle or a line – see which is easiest for you. You could use or adapt the templates below. Remember to always include 'other' as a choice.

Scales

Numbered scales can be based on either 0 to 10 or -10 to +10, depending on what you prefer

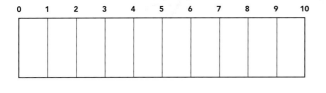

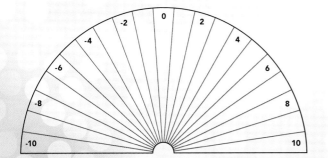

Charts (Variations)

Examples of how to use numbered charts in other ways.

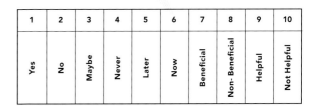

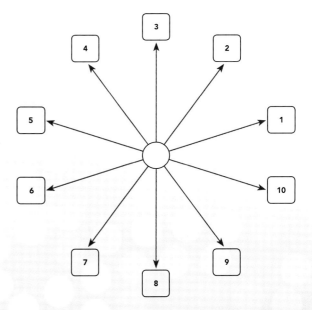

ACKNOWLEDGMENTS

Author Biographies

Nigel and Maggie Percy (authors) have been teaching and using dowsing personally and professionally since the 1990s. They are certified in Spiritual Response Therapy (SRT), a method based on chart dowsing. Maggie is a Karuna Reiki Master Teacher and Nigel a certified Spiritual Healer. Their website www.discoveringdowsing.com is the biggest repository of free dowsing training and information in the world. They are authors of over 20 books on dowsing, energy clearing and related topics, which can be seen at www.sixthsensebooks.com

Dr Patrick MacManaway (foreword) is a third generation practitioner of intuitive and healing arts, and trained first with his parents in their Healing and Teaching Centre in Fife, Scotland. A graduate of Edinburgh University Medical School, past president of the British Society of Dowsers and the author of several dowsing related books and CDs, Patrick teaches and consults with people, businesses, properties and landscape in the UK, USA and Australia.

Picture Credits

Special thanks to all the artists who have contributed artwork to this book, in page order: *Moon Tree* by © **John Sosnowsky, aka Sozra** 4; © **Klára Čmelová** 9; © **Judith Moffitt** 14; © **Meredith Nolan** 65; © **Corina Chirila** 98; © **William Adley** 101. Courtesy of **Shutterstock.com** and © **the following**: OmniArt (background throughout); robin.ph, Elchin Jafarli, Peratek (background elements throughout); Mercury Green 3, 26, 30, 48, 58, 78, 88; Benjavisa Ruangvaree Art 6, 12, 28, 64, 76, 77, 97, 105; Pixel-Shot 7; Siripong Jitchum 8; PopTika 10; Fer Gregory 11, 41; Yerko Espinoza 13; agsandrew 15, 31, 36, 40, 43, 53, 66, 69, 90, 107, 109; Dariush M 16; Alexandre Linon 22, 34; Evgeny Haritonov 23; Nikki Zalewski 24, 32, 83; Stefan Malloch 25, 93; Peratek 29, 38; Bruce Rolff 33, 114; Monika Wisniewska 35, 39, 52, 79, 86, 100; gph-foto.de 37; Zanna Lecko 42; Jozef Klopacka 44; Elena Schweitzer 45, 47, 55, 60; FotoHelin 46, 49, 57, 122; Rawpixel.com 50; frantic00 51; sutlafk 54; Juno Teo 56; S Photo 8Bit 59; Pavel_Klimenko 61; VladKK 63; Archv 68; Billion Photos 72; Phuttharak 73; LittlePerfectStock 74; Fona 75, 117; sun ok 80; watchara 82; Ganna Demchenko 84; Brian A Jackson 85; Blazej Lyjak 87; Art Furnace 89; Marben 94; Malivan_Iuliia 95, 96; pogonici 99; Stela Handa 103; Zanna Art 104; umnola 106; Veronika By 108; Iryna Kalamurza 110; Ole Schoener 111; Romolo Tavani 112; fran_kie 115; Irina Dobrotsvet 116; ueuaphoto 118; Cozine 119; Jacob_09 120; Cristina Conti 123. Courtesy of **SuperStock** and © **the following**: PhotoAlto 17; Pantheon 18, 20; World History Archive 19; Interfoto 21; ABK / BSIP 27; Cavan Images 70; Oleksiy Maksymenko / All Canada Photos 91; Alaya Gadeh / Mauritius 126.